Words From Silence

Priyanka Dixit

BookLeaf Publishing

India | USA | UK

Dedication

I want to dedicate this book to nature, the greatest and quietest teacher of consciousness. Nature neither teaches nor preaches; instead, nature dismantles our separate egos and dissolves our identities. Nature does not rely on words yet still delivers profound results. Thus, in nature without any spiritual practice, you can attain in seconds what others strive to achieve in a lifetime.

Preface

This book explores the truths we often conceal from ourselves. When we are genuinely honest, we recognize that these articles resonate with our own experiences. The pieces in this book do not focus on what we should or shouldn't do, nor are they intended to instruct anyone in any practice; rather, they invite us to embrace our own experiences as we read.

Chapter in this book are not related to each other so you can start reading any chapter instinctively.

Acknowledgements

I would like to thank my husband, Kedar Gosavi, who is the sole reason these articles are transforming into a book.

CHAPTER ONE

BREATH

From morning to evening, we are craving for identities.

Identities are different roles we play each day. When our children come in front of us we wear the identity of parents. When we are at workplace we enjoy a professional identity. When our parents are around, we live children identity. When our husband is around, we feel like a wife or when wife is around one feels like a husband. When we pray we enjoy a devotional identity with the "GOD".

From morning to night, we strive for the identities and manipulate or strategies our psychological mind to balance these identities. We love all our identities so much that we do not want to leave any of them, rather keep stacking more and more.

When we are busy in office, we do not feel our wife or parents or children identities anymore. When you have lot of bank balance you enjoy a rich identity but if you are in nature or with animals you loss or forget your rich identity. It means you are not living all the identities all the time. They fluctuate in intensity and we try to attach or detach to them as per our convenience. If we can feel the absence and presence of the identities, than we are definitely none of them, because we are continuous, cannot exist for sometime, and absent for some time. It is like having the existence and than dying.

Do you have something that is closer, continuous, and cost-free than your all the identities, or rather on which all of your identities relay?

Is there something not at all mystical but an open secret always taken for granted .Yes, it is our breath. Someone may feel now. After listening to the word 'breath', what is great in it?

OK!! Then I say, I will give you 1 billion dollar, president position, most wanted dream spouse and sweetest children, and in return, you just give me your breath.

Yes, this was the revelation I had when I focused my attention to my breath. Each and every of our breath is our existential identity itself. I am breathing that is enough and biggest gift. Recognizing this gift every moment is a bonus.

This breathing can give me contentment, which I

have never found anywhere else. Our each action, situation, identity changes have immediate reaction on our breath which in turn attack our health. If you focus on your first breath now you will observe it is always inhaling not exhale, it means we are busy stacking things in life and mind.

When we start observing our breaths, we enjoy consciously more and more exhale breath, which in turn bring relaxation and peace. Because exhale breath is sign of letting-go. It has bonus advantage, like when we start observing our breaths, we feel more relaxed and contended, we start to listen more and speak less; it gives a rich quality feeling. We learn the habit to stop. This gives us a choice to respond to the situation rather than to react. This in turn brings quality in our relationships, in our work. In addition, definitely, our health reaches to height.

Our mind is ready to believe in complex solution but miracle lies in simple and most open way for all.

Our crying, laughing, shocking, being angry, excited, sad, depressed, anxious are nothing, but different speed in which we breathe that is not a normal breath. So, just observe your breath for any outward change or news. It reduces the train, speed, and number of thoughts automatically. This saves your energy wasting in emergency thoughts.

It brings you more and more in present moment

and you feel more and more alive. You actually live. It is one of the best ways of meditation, which needs no special environment or silence.

I pray to "GOD" you live alive to your every breath. It is another words to say live your life fully.

CHAPTER TWO

BACKSEAT

In the world of hush and bush where everyone is unstoppable, it takes a huge courage to take a backseat, believe me, or not it needs both grace and faith to take a backseat.

For me taking a backseat was itself a self-experimental discovery.

Now taking a back seat does not mean to leave some big assets but very small situations in life.

Thank you "GOD" for giving the courage to take a backseat.

I will share small incidences where my mind or rather self-image tempted to jump at the top of my voice, but I preferred a backseat.

When the front person is boosting his or her self-image and making some historical story, I was tempted to speak a lot about my experiences, but I preferred a backseat and the peace and love I got from

"GOD" in bonus to show I am on right path.

When I am, alone I was tempted many a time to call someone and listen to the noise of two vocal cords talking. However, I took a backseat and discovered an enormous effortless zone of silence and patience of lifetime.

When some negative thoughts and emotions run from my body, rather than subsiding them by watching TV, Listening music, getting engrossed in some work I preferred to take a backseat and what I discovered was miraculous, every thought of my head is an illusion and has no power of its own. Moreover, thoughts no longer persist. Even if they persist it does not matter a lot because they are now like dog barking in front of the elephant where dog is voice in the head and elephant is the vast silence of which we are not the owner. Rather, it is the one we all are.

When I or my near once where suffering from illness rather than worrying I surrendered to destiny and took a backseat and experienced a struggle less, effortless and worry less zone which is hard to put in words. Nevertheless, I discovered that our body has the power to heal itself unless it is entrapped by logical thought prone remedies.

When my near once and myself do not fulfill my expectations or do not portrait as I imagine them as ideal. I used to struggle and manipulate and strategies how to change them or myself.

However, I felt this whole process very exhausting and embraced a backseat. I discovered there is an aliveness in everyone as the way they are, everyone is perfect with all the patterns and conditioning and shouldn't change until "GOD" wants' them to change. This made me relax and enjoy every person without any conflict.

This silence and loneliness I rejected initially, But the more I melted in it I can't explain what I discovered I leave it up to you to discover, But will say it is worth more than any other thing you can imagine or are running for

It initially takes efforts to have a backseat but once you start applying it one discovers its own freedom, which always existed.

CHAPTER THREE

EYES

Look at the leaf, until the leaf is no more a leaf.

Look at the sun, until you cannot define what it is.

Look at the Human beings until the time they are no more the human beings.

Eyes do not know if the sun is the sun until your mind memory comes and labels it as the sun.

Are you looking right now from the eyes or from the mind?

See who is looking through this judgment less, memoryless Eyes.
Do these eyes know your Age?

Do these eyes know Your Gender?

Do these eyes know your education or country you belong?

Do these eyes even know your NAME?

Your eyes are always here in the timeless zone but your mind makes it look through the time, through the labels and judgments'. This gives rise to an illusion that you know something about this world as everyone loves to know no one loves uncertainty or unknown. Very few are comfortable with the reality.

Your Eyes tell you how pure your looking is.

Purer the eyes,

        Transparent the scene is,

       Calmer the mind becomes,

          Fearless the emotions are,

            Life turns into love,

               Happiness becomes your eternal nature,

                  Decision comes from natural doubtless instinct.

It brings you to oneness even without knowing what oneness means.

Eyes never lie, is it looking with the label of greed, fear, anger, possessiveness, doubt, curiosity, jealousy, comparison or is it looking just because it is meant to see. Then there is no one left to look through the eyes, seeing is just happening.

If it is so easy to be timeless and spaceless, let the eyeballs be at its job without amalgamation of mind's judgment in it.

Gratitude comes for the eyes that are HERE and NOW.

CHAPTER FOUR

SENSE OF REALITY AND "WHO M I?"

Anything in life is alive until you give it a sense of
reality,
including your self-image.

When you feel anything with your five senses,
you give it a sense of reality.

The sense of reality generates fear or desires.

It then gives rise to emotions.

The basis of the sense of reality is ignorance.

Illusion

We get an illusion that there is the problem.
Then we get another illusion that there is the solution to
that problem.
And, the cycle never ends.
Unless! We realize to stop.
Everything is too perfect for our mind to realize.

Surrender

Surrender allows the awareness to percolate in your
daily routine plan and change it as it wants.

Your mind may think it is wrong, as things are not going
as per your wish, plan, or story.
Do not give up to your mind now, trust that your
individual identity is of no use to anyone.

"Who M I?"

I really do not know "who m I?" in words.
I just know that,
I constantly see desires of

"To have" and "Not to have",
"To do" and "Not to do".
Emotions, thoughts, even neutrality
Rising and falling in me.
I realize I am not my past, nor future not even present.
The biggest problem to define myself is,
I realized I could not think and find myself.
Whatever I think is an idea and created in my thoughts
and these idea and thoughts were not present before.
However, the reality is!!! "I was before the idea or the
thought; basically I was before I think."
So, I can never understand myself by thinking.
The more I settle with the unknown without words, the
more I find myself.

CHAPTER FIVE

What's Next

Have you ever noticed a bird talking to another bird, "Hey! What's next?" Have you seen a tree saying " I have improved from the last year and next year I will be greener, stronger, taller. A bud is never waiting to become a flower. A diamond never thinks that my life's purpose is to become a part of a necklace of the princess. It has the same shine in the mines as in the jewelry shop. Diamond is never sad and feels unsuccessful in the dark mines and showing off his success after being part of the exhibition mall. The Sun, The Earth, The moon are performing the same old activity from ages. Why do they never get the thought of "What's next in our life?" "What's next?" Is the bug that has bitten only to the human mind? Time really does not exist for any other species, planet, nature, or non-living things but only to the human race. Why this moment is not enough? Why are we in the hurry to end this moment and move in the next one? What is the next moment going to give you that this moment is unable to fulfill? Can we all live for diving deep in this very moment? We all cannot even imagine how our lives will be if we never get the question "what's next?" .

Do not climb the ladder of time, it is an illusion. Accept this very moment as your last one and live as you were born to live for this moment. If you are reading this article right now, feel as if this is your only purpose in life. Mind may come up with (what's next) questions like, What you will get by reading it? What is the next work you are going to do after reading it? Mind may come and say go to the kitchen its cooking time now, or it may say your life's purpose is to raise the kids, or become a millionaire, or get married or see your children getting married and settle down. The mind may also say "your life's purpose is to find the purpose of life but in the next moment or to get enlighten but in the next moment.

This is all false the truth is this is the happiest moment of your life. This moment is always the best moment. This moment will never repeat itself.

'Living every moment like it is your last one', this is the real aim of life. Then we are alive for every moment. In addition, we are not living life rather we do not have a separate life left but we are **life**.

When we are brushing our teeth, we are just brushing our teeth, not in the hurry to finish this and move into the second one. When we are having tea, we are living that moment as if we were born to have tea. All the small moments are as important as life itself. "Life is happening to you when you are busy thinking about it" this saying is so apt in this context.

You don't have the future, you don't have the past just locked in this moment and it's always going to be like this. Don't be the doer planning for life because "life takes care of life".

How is my future going to be?
What people think about me?
What is my level of consciousness?
What is my children's future?
How is life after death?
What am I going to get after doing certain work?
How much time I have studied, meditated, or worked?
What is my weight am I looking beautiful or smart?
Isn't your own self-image in the mind keeps asking such questions throughout the day? If your friends and family show that they have some information that you don't, then won't you get anxious to know what that information is? Because mind feels that, it has control and certainty if it knows about itself and the surroundings around it. Knowing, predictions and

certainty are the safety zone for the mind.

Unknown, uncertainty and non- judging makes your self-image in the mind feel vulnerable, confusing and week.

Now realize what if you do not know the answer of any of the mind's questions. Moreover, you do not wish to know the answer to any of the questions. If your instant answer is "Yes! I am completely ok with not knowing" than you are working towards your own freedom. One who starts feeling comfort in not knowing starts being free risk-free? Have faith that all you need to know will be known and all that you do not need to will never be known.

What if you accept unknown and uncertainty of every moment? The unknown is grace. If you are enjoying it than have gratitude towards this unknown, which refreshes every moment and bring aliveness and awareness to this very moment.

The need to continue....

Have you ever observed that you are dreaming early morning and it is the time to get up, but your unconscious mind is so interested to complete the dream or to see what happens next in the dream story, so it continues to watch it? Suddenly after a lot of conscious effort, your eyes open and you clearly accept that you

were dreaming. Sometimes you also get upset, that you wish you were able to see what happened next in the dream. Now when you are reading this situation you can see how foolish it is to keep thinking about a dream, which has no reality at all. Observe such need of mind to continue not only in dream but also in the daytime.
If someone meets you and discuss some economical, emotional, health-related problems, then don't you ask that person the next time he meets "has your problem resolved now?" even if the person meets you after months, you continue the conversation where you left it. If a person had a fever the day you met him, and the next time you meet him after 4 months, you ask the same question. "How is your fever now?" body heals itself every day but mentally we cannot rejuvenate. If you have animosity with someone mentally, you are forced to continue it, if you have friendship you are forced by the mind to drag it as well if it is not working organically.
Also realize the need to continue in small things, if you are talking to someone on phone and it gets disconnected due to network issue, check how your mind gets irritated or tries desperately to call again to continue the talk. When you are watching a movie and someone comes and changes the T.V channel, can you leave the movie without an erg to see what is happening in it now? When you are on specific project in the office

and suddenly shifted to a new one, won't you feel the need to continue and finish the previous project? Imagine you are reading a book at night and suddenly electricity goes, are you able to forget the book and sleep quietly. You are meditating and your child suddenly jumps on your lap, then do you get angry on him or can switch on to a new scene that God is showing you now. When you are telling your anecdote to someone and suddenly in the middle of your story the front person with whom you are having the conversation pick up his story on the same line and stop you, then don't you eagerly wait that when will he finish his talk so that I can continue?

Look at the way you try to deal with any situation. Your mind tries to continue the same solution each time. See if you just get angry to resolve any situation, or talk diplomatically every time or run away from every situation every time or just keep mum and increase your victim identity inside. This need to continue is an addiction in every field. Your awareness will show you that, you don't need to continue then the same response in all the situations. And every response can be free, new and unplanned but still perfect for the situation.

Observe your daily routine; if you have tea, do yoga or watch a specific T.V channel, you are forced to continue the same routine every day. It is not essential to watch the same T.V serial that you watched yesterday, there is no need to play the same game you played yesterday. No need to talk to the same friend you talked yesterday. The day itself is blank in the morning when you wake up, but you wish to add same activities in it, which you added yesterday. Every day is as fresh and as new life never before. If you have tea, everyday try milk, coffee or juice sometimes. Exercise patterns have no limits. Keep changing it. Dance, walk, jog, gym, cardio, yoga; every day can be a surprise for the body. You can change your food patterns so that they get hardly repeated. If you are stubborn to read specific kinds of books, you can change and taste some different categories. After all autobiography, are also fictional and fiction sometimes glances some truth. Talk to strangers, instead of sticking to the same group of friends. Change your work pattern in office and update yourself with what's new in the market to learn in your field.

Mind tries to seek "Comfort" in continuing the same pattern. And individual also sometimes take deep pride and arrogance to highlight his or her same pattern for e.g.:" I have only coffee". "I read only autobiographies". "I just like to walk". "I never accept anything for free". "I wash my face with specific soap 3 times a day". "I follow only this person", "from 40 years I have never got angry on anyone".

In reality, you should not be able to define your habits. Then there is space for GOD to fill your every day with new magic of possibilities.

Stop the "**need to continue**" and see how GOD has infinite ways to fill the blank day. And your objective look to all the activities automatically makes everything blank at night and the next day is again blank for a new fill.

RELATIONSHIPS

Sitting in silence with plants, birds, human beings and all other non-living things, I have found union with all. I can feel the presence of everything. Everything has come to life beyond its name. I have gratitude for everything to include me in them. Its relaxing, comforting and enriching. Everything in my ambience is full of life even the so-called non-living things. If this is not true relationship, then GOD knows what it is!!

In the common language when we hear the word relationship our mind pop's up with different labels like husband-wife, mother-father, sister-brother, guru-student, friends, enemies, neighbor's, colleagues. But today let's percolate the word relationship in its deepest sense so that it can be enjoyed not only on mental label but on the experiential level.

Purest definition of the word relationship is the union with your surroundings. When the word relationship comes it just tells us about two people sharing their presence with one another. When it comes to relationship of human beings with one another, there are two types of relationships. One which the universe has selected for us and wants his own universal impersonal work to get done through that relationship. These relations are divine relationships. They don't even feel like relations. Because there is no mind management involved to run these relations. These are running without any expectations, compulsions or external pressure and are not even time bound. These relations do not decrease your peace and happiness. In fact, it enhances it with an overlap of each other's, "peace and happiness."

On the other hand, there are relationships which are egocentric mind made mandatory relations, that may be blood relations, relations kept to get professional and career advancements or the dysfunctional relationships kept to fulfil each other's weaknesses. These kinds of relationships need mind management as to what to say, what not to say, what to hide, what to show. But the matter of fact is none of the parties is ever happy or at peace in each other's presence. They never increase your energy; rather your energy gets depleted more.

In the mind made relationships, even if you get what you want, it is not a one-time job. You have to keep putting the same efforts again and again. For example, if two people are in relationship because one person is scared of being left alone and always wants to be in someone's company and the other person wants someone to give a listening ear to all his or her stories and give affirmation on it. So, this kind of relationship is a dysfunctional relationship where each one is using other to protect their weakness. Here the person who cannot live alone will need to give continuous affirmation to the story of other person even whether his consciousness allows it or not. He will never be able to be completely honest to the other person. Because he knows that the moment he will speak his heart and do not give approval to the other person's story, he will be left alone.

Divine relations are not about two people having same belief systems, habits, same level of education, caliber or intellect. It is just about having two people at the same level of frequency. These people with divine relationship will automatically come in contact through unknown, unplanned and undefined events due to Grace. A saint is never comfortable in the company of a sadist or an evildoer and neither a gossip gang will love to be in the company of a silent introvert chap. Divine relations are never bored by one another or back stab one another.

There exists pure love and understanding among divine relations. They act and feel as one, not as two separate individuals. There is complete understanding and willingness to speak and share anything and everything. They don't need anything from each other in particular, but they simply cherish each other's presence. If no mind made efforts are made to keep any relationships the world will be unimaginably peaceful place to live with.

In short when all your relationships are running at the mercy of "GOD" without putting any special efforts to it, then you are having all divine relations in your life. Whereas, if all your relations need mind management, then they are definitely not working on same frequency. So, allow the divine to play its role and the mind to rest in peace.

The ultimate relationship is when there is no separate you left to have a relation with others. Then whole universe is in unison without any divisiveness and the word "Relationship" does not make any sense.

CHAPTER SEVEN

BEING YOU

Sit into a close lonely room for an hour or two without any company or electronic gadgets and enquire on this question "what is the purpose of my life?" If your mind comes and says that, your purpose is to earn money, raise your kids, become a good person, doctor, teacher or engineer or do something for the society or make this place a beautiful place to live in. Then I will say, "no, you need to percolate deeper." you have a personality which is before even you think how you should be or shouldn't be. Something, which comes naturally to you, which doesn't need effort. And this is your purpose in life, to be your natural, effortless you.

You don't need to judge yourself whether you are peaceful, happy, helping, sensitive, angry, vulnerable, fearful, or confident person.

You don't even have to think about what is your natural and effortless personality.

What is not natural for you need some struggle and effort. And you try to roll the piddle of this unnatural self in you with all the struggle and efforts only out of a sense of responsibility of not hurting someone or getting approval from someone or I should be accepted in the society or the fear of being missed out of the company, Support, money, respect, fame or something similar to it.

If sensitivity and politeness are natural to you, you don't have to feel that people will misuse you or underestimate you just because you are not a smart or angry person. On the other hand, you don't have to judge someone if being outspoken, and harsh is his or her natural nature.

If your husband or wife is outspoken, direct and you are a sensitive empath, then you both don't need to change each other. Your natural personality is neither good or bad. It works perfectly for the totality.

We make a mistake to use a natural personality to show us as superior or inferior. Being sensitive neither is good nor is being outspoken superior.

It is all the shades of one truth and works in the totality to make the elusive dance of the truth more interesting and real. Still cannot become the truth. It is like formless trying to challenge its own reality by different colors of elusive personalities but still, nothing can match the truth.

So our individual natural personalities are not

there to serve us as an individual it is to serve the totality of the universe. We have to perfectly fit naturally in the jigsaw puzzle and accept ourself as the block of the jigsaw puzzle.

You don't need to worry about our physical needs of food, clothing, shelter. These will be automatically taken care of by higher powers. Totality pays us with the gift of peace and happiness by being our true Natural Self.

So, your purpose is to be totally you. The more you be yourself, then you naturally allow and respect and love without judgment to the front person, for what he or she is.

<u>Let Everyone's Personality bloom</u>

The earth exists today, due to the varieties it conceives in its womb. The sky, plants, animals, humans, soil, flowers, mountains, and ocean make it complete and whole. If the earth is devoid of any of the elements, then it won't be the same.

Now Imagine if the ocean says to the sky, "My role is superior to yours; you should also become like me." This is hilarious, right? The role of the sky can't be compared to the role of the ocean, and if anyone starts trying to be like the other, the whole cosmos will be disturbed. Similarly, every human being has a natural personality. The personalities that are not adopted but are inborn. It's effortless for everyone.

Personalities like introvert, extrovert, empathetic, narcissistic, dominating and many more play their role and make the earth balanced in the most beautiful and loving way.

The problem starts when the comparing mind of a person starts asking which personality is superior: this or that.

All personalities have a role to play, they should be allowed to be in their destined places. An introvert can be good in research whereas a dominating personality can be a good manager but if you try to exchange their roles it will be chaos, if we want all the empathetic personalities on earth and no demanding and submissive persons; then also balance will be crumbled.

The problem starts when we feel we are individuals living for ourselves: we all on the level of the body, and the mind are given the personalities to fit in the jigsaw puzzle for Earth's manifestation.

Let our natural personality bloom then may it be introvert or extrovert. As much as we accept our personalities, we start loving and respecting everyone's personalities, instead of making it a comparison point you start getting mesmerized by a person having an exactly opposite personality to yours.

As different flowers bloom in different seasons in their

own way, the earth will be in utmost harmony when everyone shines in their natural way.

CHAPTER EIGHT

MIRACLE (WAY TO AN EFFORTLESS LIFE)

Miracle is not to get what you want. Miracle is to forget what you want.
Miracle is not in getting a billion dollar lottery, But miracle is when every little action of the day start feeling as miracle as brushing your teeth or looking the face in the mirror or tying the knot of your shoes.
Every step you walk seems like a miracle.

flow of life

Have you ever experienced all your daily activities happening effortlessly and passionately simultaneously? These activities may be your job, hobby, or daily chores. Then you are in the brain's zone called the flow of life. The flow of life seems to be a philosophical term but it is a state of mind. It is an egoless state so it seems philosophical. In this state mind completely focuses its attention on the activity at hand. Being able to enter the state of flow is emotional intelligence at its best. Have you ever felt that even if your job doesn't pay you, just doing it is worth all the spontaneous joy it brings in the moment? Then you are in the flow of life. The mind has two states the one which is always thinking of "I (me, Myself)" This part of the mind is also called the "ego" which is always concerned about what I am going to get by doing this work. This is a very effortful place to be, as your "me" thoughts are making monkey dance and don't allow you to focus and loosen yourself in the moment even for a few seconds. And the other part of the mind is not concerned with my thought, this is a mind free to immerse in the present activity. This mind takes you in the effortless flow of life.

If a painter is painting just for the joy of painting, then it is easy for him/her to go in the flow state. This happens because he/she has no thought of how much this painting will be sold for, or will people like it or not. These thoughts cause anxiety to the mind and distracts the brain.

Studies by famous psychologist Howard Gardner in his theory of multiple intelligence state that the healthiest way to teach kids to tap their inner natural talent easily is in the state of flow rather than forcing them by fear or rewards. Flow Is an internal positive state that states the kid is engaged in the right task. Most of the top athletes, artists and scientists perform their best in this state. Flow is the prerequisite for mastering any art, craft and learning. If you are reading the book and the mind is distracted, feeling bored, or rejecting to read, and you still keep reading the book for 15 minutes you will come to a flow state where the brain's neural activity in the natural zone and your concentration reach to its peak so that even two hours of reading feels timeless.

In flow, you are in an ecstatic state to such a point that you feel you do not exist. You are living without yourself and have nothing to do with what is happening. You are in a state of awe and wonderment of things happening through your body and mind effortlessly. If your brain is trained to be in this state even whole life becomes timeless and spaceless.

Way to an effortless life

Was life really effortless from the beginning? Putting effort is making obstacles to the flow of divine effortless life which is beyond anyone's imagination.

See people jumping around to make their lives perfect. No one has a second guess what if it is perfect already? Correct thinking, Strategizing is not making life perfect or beautiful or worth living. Relaxing, Letting the moment unfold itself and ready to see it as it is, diving into uncertainty is coming alive to life.

Relaxing is not the art of becoming lazy. But in fact, seeing your body unfolding its action before any planning and enjoying the creativity which is seen by the mind itself for the first time. This makes the mind surprised more if it is honest and allows itself to drop more and relax more. Your body may end up doing happily and interestingly ten more things it could have imagined of. But that is not really what we are looking for. Counting and taking credit for the actions done or not done is again a trap.

You beautifully and gracefully relax and let the scenes flow. Don't try to make any formula, what has worked this time may not necessarily work other times as well. GOD throws an apple pie on the face when the mind feels it knows it all! like how to influence people, how to earn money, how to be healthy, how to win GOD :), How to get self-realization, and peace and happiness.

Juggling with time is another misconception, if every moment is handled on its own, time is an illusion. If you stop mentioning time as day and night will the sun won't rise or set? If you don't make a lot of effort to pass the day it will still slip smoothly like butter. Putting a lot of effort is just a sign of a mind not being able to view and be one with life as it is. It is actually not being comfortable with yourself because you are life after all. God has given every mind the power of imagination and planning but the execution of every moment is kept in his hands only. As we hear people say "a leaf won't move without GOD's permission". Wise is the one who understands this fact and stops imagining or planning. Then his and GOD's wish becomes one and he flows effortlessly merrily merrily merrily!!!! Because now life is not a dream 😊 for him anymore.

Let the "*Truth*" unfold

The Truth has nothing to do with your individual personal story.

It brings the situation in life and starts revealing itself. When your body is free of your story, Truth reveals the fact as it is. Truth uses such bodies to unfold.

When Truth reveals itself, there is no credit taker for the good actions or bad actions. Actions and words are simply based on facts and no one is interested in its profit and loss.

No one is judging the actions, events, and situations; so, have gratitude for everything in life.

Nothing happens by mistake; nothing is wrong or unavoidable. What needs to happen will happen, what does not need to happen will never happen.

Let the truth reveal itself without allowing your 'Sins' and 'Virtues' to intervene in It.

CHAPTER NINE

VICTIM -BEST PLACE FOR THE EGO TO HIDE

What are your thoughts about the ego, the one that is showing off its superiority and trying to dominate others? The one who strives hard to show off all its real or bluffing achievements? But no, it is not the only place for the ego to survive. In fact, it is an effortful place for the ego to be.

 The effortless place of ego to be alive is as the victim. The victim's thoughts are like; "I am so poor child on the earth and all the bad things happen to me". "People come and use me", "I get drained up", "Why GOD test me only and so many stories; they are easy to construct and easier to believe and repeat again and again till the point they start feeling true.

 Ego is a shapeshifter; it is a form that does not exist but for it to be alive we need the ego to keep giving shape. Like a cloud is just the face of water but still, we give it a different name. Similarly, ego is a thought powered by consciousness to make a delusion of a separate existence. This existence may be in the form of superiority or inferiority.

Be careful of the victim identity, it is easy to be formed for which you do not have to do anything.

Once a wise sage said, "Ego will love to be a rotten egg but will not accept, that it does not exist."

Being in the power of your own self makes you realize you are beyond any form. You don't need the support of superiority or inferiority. Because who is other than you who really exists. If no one exists then with whom to compare.

The stories in the head are cloud balloons. Don't inflate it. Let them pass.

 "Be in your formless nature and enjoy the dance."

<u>Heart and Head</u>

It may seem like the fight of mind and heart.
The heart is ever ready to be open
to encompass everyone, to listen to anyone or to speak
to anyone.

The mind has all manipulation, the right and wrong concepts.

Nevertheless, believe it; it is better to go through the ticking of the mind and letting it shout at the top of your voice in your head and still doing what heart says.

Soon you will realize voice in your head is nothing and has no power and it cannot do anything

except disturbing your inner image of who you think you are and not the real Who You Are.

<u>Hell, and Heaven</u>

doer-ship, claiming that I have done this is hell and non-doer ship, not claiming credit for things that are done realizing they just happened is heaven. I recently experienced hell after a long time. And then contemplated on what was the difference between outside and inside.

From outside my life was the same, getting up, doing workouts, cooking, reading, writing, playing music, playing with kids. But still, someone was restless everywhere. And how can I get rid of that someone who was restless?

So, what I got to know was that, when there was a feeling of heaven, I was doing the same activities from outside which I was doing when feeling like hell.

This made one thing clear the outer activities were never causing heavenly feelings or hell-like feelings to be experienced on the body.

The only difference was there is no inner separate story going on with an individual from last one year and from last five days I could feel that there is an individual who has the story and that story started running in the background of each activity of the day.

For example, previously when I was brushing my teeth, only the action of brushing was going on, there was no separate individual in the background who was saying, Oh !! how is my day going to be, I am a very nice person, what happened in past, what will happen in future. Only the action of brushing the teeth was going on and it was complete in itself, fresh and new, and going on in space. Similarly, cooking, studying, talking in sessions, playing are just actions going in space they are not going on with a back story.

The backstory is the problem. While doing the same actions, from last 5 days backstory started, Oh !! this is how I am, how others are, how is my future, what I told, what others told and so on...; This "SO ON.." is going to overshadow the actions that are going on right now and create hell.

If the action of reading is happening, then that reading will not matter to me, whereas the background story will be more important and this will bring hell like feeling. The feeling of heaven resumed again when slowly I understood that the story in the background is making

me something which I am not, and realizing myself as
Nothing and Zero brings back heaven.

All the actions are again happening in space and are
complete in themselves with no background story in it.
So, the moral is when you **are the life** you are heaven
and when you **have the life** you are hell.

CHAPTER TEN

MISFIT EVERYWHERE IS BEST FIT ANYWHERE

If you think that you are a person who is misfit everywhere then you are the best candidate to become the fittest everywhere.

Sit relax and see why you are the misfit in any group.

A group or flocks of people together are always sharing something common. For examples, old people share the same health or family issues, teenagers have the same interests in movies, sports or problem from parents, women are together discussing children or household topics. Men talk on politics or economics. People of different age group also come together because they want to share the same beliefs of religion, country, spirituality, psychology or knowledge about a specific profession or education. People with no same belief also come together because they share the same belief that "they need a company".

Therefore, from all the above scenarios you must have got that if you are unable to fit anywhere, it means you do not have any strong belief system and that is the good NEWS. When you do not have any strong belief within you, you cannot define yourself easily. This makes you broadminded easy going anywhere. You are most comfortable with your own company and simply be the invisible company of any group.

You can be the one who openly hears and listen to all but neither agrees nor disagrees with anyone.

This makes you the perfect fit anywhere without conflict.

CHAPTER ELEVEN

FILLING THE VOID

Just the time we open our eyes each morning, we are starting a fight against time which is also created in our head.

Our mind asks us every moment indirect question of "How to fill the void?" and we are at its best service.

Most of the people don't even want to invest the time every day in deciding what to do. Hence, they plan all the weekdays, every hour very tightly. Even the weekends are planned well in advance.

All this "struggle", just, not to fall into the void.

The ones who are free of goal are also busy every moment deciding what to do, either gossip on phone or in person, watch TV, read books, play games, stock on social media or search for a work or pastime techniques.

All this struggle just to fill the void.

If you are trying to fill the void continuously this means void is present all around with or without time, without your struggle to even bring it or save it or maintain it.

If this void is ever present, then isn't it possible that this void is you and the one trying to fill it, is your illusionary image?

So, experience What is the reality

Is the

Void = your/our/everyone's internal nature

Struggler filling the void = illusionary mind made self-image.

Time= illusionary tool(net, trap) to keep the struggle going

Every moment mind tries to put us on a journey of desires. It wants to put us on some marry-go-round trip. It will never settle with the present moment.

Moment by moment life goes like this and we are not at
all inclined to know what can be changed in our life and
our routine.
We need to add minutes of relaxation to our activities.
Just note the unneeded activities, talk, thinking that goes
on all day. You will put on some journey.
Most of the activities of the day are useless, talk almost
useless and thoughts useless.
Sit and introspect yourself and try to understand the
DNA of your body and mind. It needs to come into the
present moment for no good reason.

Change your activities; just sit for some time with
yourself without any activities. You will realize that you
are not missing on anything.

CHAPTER TWELVE

HORIZONTAL OR VERTICAL LIFE

There are two types of life you can live. One, you have a life and second, you are life. When you are living a horizontal life, you have a goal, you have continuity and you have a life. When you are living vertical life, you do not have a life rather you are life, you do not have a goal you are the goal.

What happened five minutes before and what will happen five minutes after is important in horizontal life. But what is happening now is only important in vertical life. What happened five minutes before is garbage and what will happen five minutes after is just imagination or illusion in vertical life.

When you want to control your life and live a planned and known life, it may be a monotonous but known life.

Things may not give the results from the past ten years but you keep doing the same thing because it is known, it is a habit and all you know is horizontal life. You read a lot, listen a lot and know a lot of concepts. For example, eating salad will make you healthy is what your mind has read, but is it really giving the results is not explored. You got a readymade answer and solution and you bought it as true and you keep following it blindly without going into the unknown and doing its research. Because in horizontal life everything is in time and in time you are always short of time.

Whereas in vertical life, all the readymade answers are rejected. You don't know what is working and why. But you are flowing in life and every moment is unknown but alive and is revealing itself. With this awareness, you will know what every bite of salad is doing to your body right now. Is it giving you a health or just mental satisfaction - everything is explored from the unknown and by the unknown. And everything here happens for the first time. Every time you read anything you read it for the first time, As it has no relation with the past. Every time you cook it's now the first time and you feel the excitement and aliveness it brings with it.

The biggest difference between horizontal and vertical life is! you have a goal horizontally and that Is why it is horizontal or continuous but in vertical life, you are the goal. let us understand this with an example, if you are running 5 miles a day, the goal in continuous life will be that of comparison. Yesterday I completed 5 miles in 40 minutes and today I will complete it in 30 minutes. But in the case of vertical life, if you are doing yoga, the stretching felt every moment in yoga is experienced in awareness for the first time and that is enough, what result you will get out of it is not at all important.

Most important in continuous horizontal life is the need for your psychological self to be alive. In fact, if you are not in time, not in comparison with the past and future, then there is no oxygen for your self-image of yourself in your head. It's a psychological death!! Vertical life is not the slave of the psychological self. It does not have a self-image. You know you are alive as you are NOW. Untouched by any story or autobiography. As horizontal life is in time, you experience all the opposites in life - boredom-excitement, success-failure, you-me, past-future and so there is Burdon on your face all the time, the conflict of all the opposites. But when you are vertical life, you are free of any Burdon, untouched by opposites and being in the unknown allowing every moment to reveal itself. And allowing it to pass peacefully as it is. You just flow and flow and flow with all your autobiographical pages blank as you are writing on the water where no imprints of a person are seen. In horizontal life, 10 empty minutes seem like 100 years and in vertical life, 100 years seem like a second.

Doing as Being

Being is the doing that is not thought of as doing before, during, or after performing the activity; That is why it is relaxing timeless doing. You never feel tired as your body is doing but your mind is not recording it in time and space.

Body and mind are meant to work but not to take credit for it. Then working is fun and something you are not looking to complete or escape.

See the small activities of the day like reading, eating, writing, cooking, bathing, brushing, etc., Don't perceive them as means to an end but something your life is looking forward to. Every small activity of the day is happening in your being and so it is alive only till the time you are doing it and ends with no trace of the work done except in your memory from where you say "Oh, you know I did gardening for 4 hours today." This memory is garbage, and if at all it has any .0001% of use "GOD" will use it from your brain, you don't have to keep remembering or marketing the activities done by your body. And this is all you need to know. Then being is life and life is being with every activity in it as non-active relaxed doing.

CHAPTER THIRTEEN

WORDS

Words come first or you?
Words are the labels to divide the oneness
Let us play the game of words
Just give me some words from your thinking pocket and
see the magic where you fall or find yourself right now.

Give me the word "Time"
Now tell me, where you are?

Give me the word "Place"
Now tell me, where you are?

Give me the word "My"
Now tell me, what is yours?

Give me the word "Me"
Now tell me. "Who you are"?

Give me the word "World"
Now tell me, what is left?

Stop Labeling morning, afternoon, evening and night
Stop Labeling Sun, Moon, Stars, Planets, Galaxy, Country
& City

Words are just the labels to hide unbreakable infinite
stillness.

Everyone can make the other superior or inferior just in
words.

Once we know this subconsciously, words losses its
power over you.

You do not know your own power.

You are the one cannot be labeled by words.

You are beyond words.

Realize and enjoy this good NEWS.

Don't still try to search yourself through words.

CHAPTER FOURTEEN

BE AWARE OF WHAT YOU EXCHANGE

Stop judging, speculating, strategizing, planning, managing and manipulating for small pity things like,

Winning an argument,

Shinning your superiority,

Fighting for your existence

Proving yourself to be right

Alternatively, getting some goals achieved

If you are still interested in these things, it is your wish.

Nevertheless, mind well,
You are exchanging Kohinoor diamond for garbage bin,
because you are exchanging your silence for noise.

However, yes, it is true:
This will be possible only when you have melted in your
own silence.

Running in life or walking as life

Running in life is full of the baggage of right or wrong,
every moment one is confused to take a right turn or left
turn leap backward, or move forward. And no matter the
turn one takes, judgments about other pathways will
keep him bound to which was right and which was
wrong. Many faces are seen from morning to night of
this confusion.
But few faces are also seen where life has stopped
as "My life" and every moment only **walking as life** is
happening. There is no right or wrong, there is only
grace and intimacy towards life. Every scene is
experienced with utmost romance and respect as if it
was meant to be. Deeply absorbing with complete
surrender to every moment is their mantra.
There are no "Ifs and buts" just flowing thinner than air,
every move of life is experienced as never experienced
before and will never occur again. But the paradox is

that no matter how intimately this moment is experienced the next moment it's garbage for the one **walking as life**. Because for him the only thing that ever matters is this moment, not a mile before nor a mile after.

"Running in life" is bound by the karmic accounts of nature. It's in time and space. Every such face is never contented because there is no understanding of the mystery.

When one starts **walking as life** it becomes a **mystery**. A moment may be joyful or sorrowful, of pride or guilt, or of kindness or cruelty never judged only experienced by the mystery, this is walking as life. **"WALKING AS LIFE"** is about experiencing everything intimately but no imprints ever formed and the pages of the autobiography are blank even though it's the only one who lives the life **fully.**

Live life completely

When I say, "Live life completely", then most of the minds will pop up with their unfulfilled dreams to be completed.

Unfulfilled dreams mean adventurous sports, dancing, getting married, having children, dancing, shouting, scolding, wearing certain dresses, having dreams house, car, traveling to your dream places, watching TV or listening to music as much as you want. Alternatively, it may mean getting a dream job, should have as much money in the purse as much you want to shop, playing all of your favorite games.

Some minds on the constructive and positive side may feel that live life completely means, "To complete some unimaginable work before one dies, to make a discovery, to make a mark in history. To change this world or make it a better place to live for next generation, to strive every bit of the day doing some work and making full use of the day."

Nevertheless, this is not all that I am speaking about or pointing to when I say, "Live life completely". It means whatever I am doing or not doing I am completely in the moment.

If I am having a cup of tea, I am enjoying every sip of it as if I am having it for the first time and will never have it again. If I am talking to someone then it is as if I have infinite time to be with that person. If you are listening to someone, you feel so complete that you become the ear. If you are just sitting, you may ask, Can I get as relaxed as possible while sitting. If you are cooking you are engrossed with all your senses of enjoying every bit of cooking. If you are working on your laptop, you are in a timeless zone regardless of what will the result of any action you are doing. Doing anything itself becomes so much fun that it feels like non-doing. Every work is no more a work. You start drinking every day with the straw made by each of your breath. You do not need to add adventure into your life anymore, on the other hand, life itself becomes adventurous, even if from outside it may feel like you are doing any simple or rather no activity.

On the contrary, can you also start living all the so-called negative aspects of life? For example, if someone said, a lot bad about you or proved you wrong, some dreams are not coming true. Can you understand how you feel or how your body-mind reacts to it? Can you allow your body to feel it without making a fast effort to change it? Allow It to be completely be felt. Can you enjoy the life as it is? May be you can or maybe not, But what is the risk in giving it a shot.

When you start living your life fully, your life starts to be simpler. The dept in your life will start to increase; you will be ready to see whatever life wants' to show you, rather than making a continuous effort of push and pull.

Dept in life, increasing in gratitude, satisfaction, patience, forgiveness, love and peace in any situation are all by-products or are fruits of being fully ready for life as it is.

You are not trying to be desire less but you enjoy any bit of life as it is. When you are not able to find wrong in any situation you do not need for any special situation. In addition, your decisions at every step are now from the deeper place of life rather than which happed earlier only by thinking some profit and loss.

Do not try to prove the whole world how much fully you are living your life completely. Your presence will speak for itself, even if it does not who cares.

CHAPTER FIFTEEN

BEHIND THE CURTAINS

One projects another person's life behind the curtains of the mind and assumes it to be true.

Imagine you are standing on one side of the curtain and another person is on another side. If the person on the other side laughs or say WOW!! You get curious to know what is there behind the curtain, which I am not able to experience and the other person is.

In reality, no one is getting anything. Our day starts with an empty hand and ends empty-handed.

During the day, whatever experiences a person is getting, may be good, excellent, happy, sad; all are momentary and is going to end.

No experience lasts forever.

If a person loves to have the experience of traveling, then he can enjoy it 5 days, 10days max a year. Then that experience ends and remains just in the form of memory. Holding the experience in memory is like keeping the stale food in the fridge and avoiding the fresh new memoryless present available to breathe.

If one is allowed to speak about his experiences without touching his memory, one will be left empty handed with a void.

This is reality of everyone, but recognizes someone and accepts hardly anyone.

CHAPTER SIXTEEN

WORLD DEPENDS ON YOUR THINKING

Every individual is working as per his or her 'mind world'. But have you ever really questioned yourself - does this world really exist? We fear to question this because, it will remove our world from us, leaving no place to stand, not even space of air to stand.

When you think of the sky then it exists, where is the sky until that time? When you think of your parents, spouse, children then they exist, where are they until then. When you think of "time" then it exists, where is the time until then. When you think of yourself, you exist where are you until then.

The existence of everything is in your head. I am no one if I do not think. However, we are not ready to lose our pseudo image because that makes us feel we do exist.

When "NOW" is touched by the senses then mind creates a world. This World created by mind in "Now" is the play of GOD and is part of happening. For example, when you look at the rose your mind comes and labels it as rose and gives it an adjective as beautiful and the rose becomes beautiful. In short, world becomes beautiful. You get the feeling that there is one "YOU" who is watching the rose. Meaning, mind has come and made three things by thinking. One is 'You', who is watching the rose, second is rose the object that is being watched and the third is the act of watching. If the mind did not say anything, you will not have any division of content (YOU, Rose and Watching) and there is only oneness; only emptiness.

This mind created content, once understood, will not divide you anymore. In addition, you will get the reality that you are not part of the content but apart from it. Now the illusion for me at this moment is that I am writing an article. However, it is ok for this moment as it allows the play of "GOD" for this moment to be played but it has no reality in my head. After some time, this NOW will have Kitchen and cooking action in it. So, at that time in the kitchen, the reality of writing the article does not exist anywhere except in the mind memory as a past action. That time, unless I think, I will not be able to create this scene of one "me" writing the article in the balcony with cool evening breeze flowing and the sun setting slowly.

By this time, we understood how the mind creates a world of contents and division in the NOW with the help of senses - that is by seeing, hearing, smelling, touching, or speaking and it is ok to let the play of "GOD" happen. Slowly we will understand that its only purpose is to know that NOW exists and we are nothing but this "NOW".

There is another world, which is created which is not at all part of "NOW" or has nothing to do with the contents of "NOW". As discussed earlier when this reality of writing the article will be finished it will have no place other than in my memory. It means, the scene of 'writing the article' cannot be created unless I think about it. So now, suppose you are in the kitchen and you have utensils, cooking ingredients, and gas stove in front of you. At this time there is no office, spouse, relatives, and friends in this scene. Therefore, mind is in pure action of cooking. This is a simple mind, simple fake world, and simple reality in "NOW". Then suddenly you start thinking "Oh! Yesterday my office colleagues were going out for dinner and they didn't invite me." In reality, this world of office has no reality, but your thinking suddenly creates this world of office, colleagues and dinner. Now you understand what I mean when I say, "World depends on our thinking".

When the action of cooking is going on there is no "YOU" who is working in the office. So, there is no question of your colleagues or their bonding with you. Just by thinking, you created a "YOU" who works in the office which triggered the thought of colleagues and your relationship with them. All this is thinking. Therefore, it is illusion. The mind when it creates this world which is not the part of NOW is a complex mind and has no reality at all. Not even in the play of GOD.

Even if you think of a scene in the past or imagine a situation in the future, which was or will be beautiful, blissful, and full of respect and achievement, it is completely fake, since it is created by your mind. Positive or negative thinking both are illusions if not part of the NOW.

Your complex mind has no role anymore once you accept that you have no interest in a fake world. Therefore, the whole world vanishes and only simple world remains of contents of NOW. You use this simple mind as a beautiful tool to innovate in the NOW and GOD does fill the color of happening in the non-happening NOW.

Slowly you start seeing the content of "NOW" is mind created. Therefore, it is good for play but has nothing to do with YOU. You come to realize you are the Pure NOW always where the mind writes the contents and vanishes again by time. You are the Now like blackboard on which mind as a chalk keeps writing and creating the world, time is the duster, which rubs the content all over again. Blackboard was black all the time, and empty which is its inherent nature. Realize your own truth, which does not need the world that depends on your thinking. It is easy to understand, simpler to experience but very difficult to accept as it ends not only your world but "THE WORLD!"

Think and lose

When you "THINK," you distance yourself from your true self.

"OH! My yesterday was so wonderful!", "In 6 months, I will see my children.", "Was I impressive in the meeting yesterday?", "I am a good person, but people do not understand me.", "What are they thinking about me?", "There is some misunderstanding between us."

All these thoughts create a web of thinking, causing you to lose your real self, which is "NOW."

Here and now, you are alive without thought.

Thinking about the present moment is always nonjudgmental and simple, much like cooking in the present requires thoughts about the recipe being

prepared; this type of thinking is called simple thinking.
However, when thinking occurs without purpose in the
present, it becomes ego-driven or complex unconscious
thinking. It merely serves to keep the separate self alive,
which is a thought.

'Intuition,' 'wisdom,' and 'intellect' all thrive in the
"NOW" and have no role in thinking. Thinking pulls you
away from these powers and traps you within itself,
offering no solutions at all.

Thinking is a small tool best used for performing present
activities or solving real practical problems. Beyond that,
it's a complete waste of energy. Yet, this is the real fear:
the moment you cease unwanted thinking, your
psychological death occurs, and the continuous void,
which is your true self, is all that remains. But sadly, you
are unaware of your real self. And the paradox goes on
forever to avoid the void {The real you} and clinging to
thinking {illusionary you}.

CHAPTER SEVENTEEN

"Divine plan is the "Zone"

Whatever may be the pattern of anyone's life, then may it be a beggar on the street or a business man ranked first in the country; everyone is leaning the day towards avoiding the pain and indulging into pleasure. These pleasures are sometimes mistaken as happiness. But that is altogether different topic to be discussed later on.

Now the question is why we indulge in pleasures and avoid pain. Everyone knows sugar has zero nutritional value, then why are there so many profits making dessert shops around the world.

The answer is simple. Our brain releases some kind of chemicals when our senses are filled with the desired content. Like; when ears hear praise, eyes see loved ones, tongue tastes delicious food, Skin feels comfortable weather. All these things are considered by the brain as positive and so it releases a chemical that is giving you the feeling of normality. This is 3D world and almost the whole world is aware of this. They may not be aware of why they do what they do. But they do for the same reason.

 Now other than this 3D sensory dimension, there is another dimension that is simpler, clearer, available for all.

This dimension takes you in the zone which has power of Joy, Happiness and peace, that is unexplainable. Yet it is accessed by only a few.

When you go beyond profit and loss you access this. When you surrender yourself to this moment and allow the moment to use you. You get connected to a "Zone" which is getting connected to the universe with no individual identity left. Your body, actions you are doing like working on computer, in office, cooking, cleaning, meditation, talking, and the work itself become one. You do not have a separate identity left. Your being is dancing one with universe. You have lost yourself now who will be in profit and who will be in loss.

There is no blueprint or a carbon copy of yours left to be added in your autobiography. So no more horizontal life. It is vertical, vertical and vertical. With zero footsteps being made.

Love is life then life is love. This zone is available for everyone to taste and free of cost and not graced on a few. But the paradox is still rare is the one who gulps it all.

Everyone wants to know their purpose of life. But there is no such thing as one purpose of life. It unfolds Moment by Moment. True purpose is to let your body be freely used by "**Self**" for its expression to flow every moment.

Now how we will come to know that what you are doing is your divine plan or the ego centric goal driven activity. **It's simple**; when we have nothing to do with the results of the activity and everything is happening in flow and takes you in a "**zone**" it is a divine plan. You are not even finding the need to take credit of the actions happening through you. The actions which come from your body and it'-s doing itself gives you happiness, then it is divine action, that is your divine plan in the moment. Like this, divine plan is not something you will come to know 5 years ago or 5 minutes ago, it happens in spontaneity in the moment and takes a creative form from the uncertain place.

Any action which has nothing to do in comparison to another person not even your self is your divine plan. It takes you to a **zone** which is a different dimension which is different from this 3D world.

We can never judge a person from the actions he/she is performing whether his/her actions are coming from a divine place or from the personal space. Same actions can be personal or divine. When I am painting and not having any other thoughts like "I want to show this painting to the world", "Will my painting be sold," "Is it better than some other person's painting or my own old ones", Then it is a divine action.

Similarly, you get up in the morning at 4' AM and even look at the clock and recognize it's 4 am still simply getting up is joy for you then it is your divine plan. But on the other hand, if you take effort to get up at 4 am and want to have pride in it. It's happening from a personal place and will not give you that same joy but rather a bit of pressure and pleasure which will have smell of the person.

If cooking is your divine plan in the moment, then it will take you to the different world in the dimension different from this 3D world. **The joy and happiness in this zone are not explainable in words**. And as soon as that action is over, you forget it because your next divine plan is ready in the current moment. You don't have anything to show to anyone from the past. As you are busy immersed in the sanity of this moment and the action as expression of this moment from you. Hence you cannot have an autobiography or a story to let others know when you are on your divine plan. Just the joy and happiness keep increasing as it has no limits. This joy and happiness add up the peace in your life, and its beauty is so deep that you never feel like taking pride or describe or perform any of your actions for some result. You yourself will never want to talk about it to others. Blowing your own trumpet will feel like an effort and give very ugly taste.

Our divine plan is never an action which is performed to take revenge, show someone down, make ourself feel superior. It's just happening for the sake of happening. Your reading, playing music, workout, cooking, technical work, cleaning the house, talking or listening to someone, meditation, dance, studying, singing, mundane clerical documentation work, investment related activities can be your divine plan in the moment if it has nothing to do with blocking any other person's divine plan or assuring you of some future results.

Most of the people do workout and diet to either look attractive or have a good health, but no one can imagine that the same actions can be performed because it is giving happiness in the moment. Body muscles stretch during workout in itself is extremely joyful and it does not want any other result from it in future. Diet makes you feel that body is saying thank you in the moment. If you get any result from it in future it's just a bonus but was not your goal.

Doing something for someone, giving a listening ear sometimes, **"leaving"**- what's not coming effortlessly towards you and **"gracefully accepting"** what is given to

you, this is divine plan as it is above any profit and loss. GOD! use this body every moment as per your divine plan and the Joy, Happiness and peace you give in return is more than enough to breath. In fact, I cannot expect any more. It is beyond my dreams and thinking.
Let everyone discover their divine plan in the moment and experience the joy, peace and happiness which is a **zone** in itself.

CHAPTER EIGHTEEN

SENSITIVITY & MATURITY

Sensitivity is felt when we start to speak less both from inside as well as outside and start to feel things without question, without reason and without the mental curiosity to find the answer of anything.

The rainy season is so calm and relaxing, just feel it and be one with it, why do you want to put efforts to know the reason why rain is so rejuvenating. If feelings are available quietly why to intervene with it.

Sensitivity increases when you speak less and listen more, guide less and get the guidance more. Not from the outside world but from the silent inner voice which wants to express joy, love and maturity through your body.

Sensitivity is not to solve anyone's problem, but to sense how this world is already so perfect that it never had the problem. Sense the perfection, the completeness and the actions happening. All are happening from a very sensitive place.

I am back into action but still all the actions feel like no action that is being back into myself. See and talk to every little non-living thing near you. Everything says thank you, when you take care of that. Not in the hurry to complete anything not in the hurry to understand anything just go slow. Allow the love to be sensed and flow and sense the integrity of this moment, rest will follow.

As your sensitivity increases you see how life guides itself. How everything falls in place so beautifully, every thought that comes need your complete ignorance they are not running your life, but just illuding you. And this you is itself a thought.

Sensitivity proved love is life and life is love. Sensitivity Is to look into vacuum from the vacuum. Where the nothingness is being the truth of the hour. This writing, the pen, the paper and the one who is writing seems to come from a blackhole. Where are you to understand anything there is no separate individual to take actions to do any actions. Still actions are happening and wisdom is evolving.

More the sensitivity increases you come to know no one is there to choose to perform an action, to understand anything.

Sensitivity gives wisdom to see how I talk and I Create, I perceive and my world is created.

Sensitivity towards time make you know I create past, present and future in the NOW which is before time.

Time is just a thought, because I am NOW and the past, present and future dance in front of me.

Sensitivity is to have patience and trust the universe the way it wants to unfold every day and see the magic of your not planning, pushing or controlling the things to happen this way or that way. It is as amazing as it can be. Trust your feelings not your thoughts, this will make you sensitive towards your intuitive guidance and your divine plans.

Maturity,

The art to release the control is maturity. See during the day on how pity things you want your control. The food I am going to eat, what people around me should say, Do, and even think, which work in my to-do list is most urgent and need to be done now.

I am not here to prescribe any remedy of how to lose the control because that will be another controlling effort to lose control.

During any moment, just ask yourself can you let go of this desire and still keep your happiness intact. As soon as the desire appears, just hear the inner voice within you that says, let go of this wish, it is very pity desire than knowing the deeper truths.

Moreover, letting go means that you are letting go of yourself. And, grace will make you leave it. In addition, you will be free from many conflicts, desires, and confusion.

Maturity is a deep breath in the present and letting go of your story.

CHAPTER NINETEEN

SIMPLICITY: --> WAY TO AWAKENING

All the persuasions of the individual are seen as very complicated by the mind. Most of the population agrees it's a lot of effort to get educated, earn money, raise kids, get a healthy body or get anything you aim for.

Mind makes all kinds of planning & strategies for getting all that it longs for. It is honest sometimes and dishonest sometimes. Argues with himself about the compromises he made to reach the desired dream.

If outer living is perceived to be so complicated, what mind must be thinking about self-realization? The mind thinks it will take millions of lifetimes to reach the self-realization state. And if he is on this path then it makes lots of projects and methods to reach to awakening.

But the paradox is awakening is simpler than the word "SIMPLE".

Simplicity can be one of the easiest pointers to self-knowledge. There are a few activities of the day that every individual needs to do but are never given importance. The chores like making your bed, brushing, bathing, eating, all these activities are to be performed by everyone; "rich or poor", but rare is the one who will have it as the goal of life.

When these small unescapable activities of the day are respected and lived with utmost care without taking them as the means to an end, an aperture or gate opens which was ever-present. This door then brings you in "NOW", the timeless dimension. Peace and happiness are cherished here effortlessly and relaxation is a bonus.

So, pay attention to chores you cannot escape. For example, working on the laptop is for an individual's goal but after finishing the work, cleaning the laptop, spreading your hand on it with love and gratitude and then keeping it in a laptop bag will bring a presence of mind. The mind may come up "Oh! I am getting late to go to play or want to see updates on what's app". Ignore your mind and end the work with dignity by keeping all tools at the respected place.

After coming from the office or school, place your shoes in the right location and bag in the closet. After finishing your writing put the books and pen in the right location. Cleaning, watering plants and similar small activities bring serenity to you.

You are not slowing down your life, you start to live life. This brings you to a magical, simple and rich life you have never dreamt of.

Purpose of life

The purpose of life is life itself. We all have so many expectations from life. But when we see it from the lens of aliveness, we love it as it is.

When we no longer search for anything to fulfill our lives, we are already living the purpose of life. When we achieve anything, we wish to share it with the world. We look for approvals and appreciation. But when we are so emotionally satisfied within, we are not looking for anything outside of us. What we are doing is itself fulfilling and simple. It does not need recognition from anyone not even feel the need to share it with anyone then it's the purpose of life.

CHAPTER TWENTY

EARTH IS NOT A SHOPPING MALL

We can observe ourselves from morning to night. Are we not acting as if we are in a shopping mall? We desire some things, reject others, and wish to exchange a few. "I am in the shopping mall of Earth," is a subconscious thought for every individual.

No? You're not getting it? Okay, let's see. We seek promotions at work, a spouse with a list of qualities, or children with the genes of Einstein. We want to explore the world and acquire luxurious houses and cars. Or the opposite the new trend is to embrace a minimalist lifestyle, living in nature or in small, underdeveloped rural areas. But beyond material possessions, we also crave respect, recognition, and fame; we want to appear eternally youthful and be seen as the most virtuous individuals. We maintain a small shopping list throughout the day, but in addition, we desire good friends and family—essentially, we want meaningful relationships.

These are the things we want, but there is a long list of things we do not want: not to be insulted, no untrustworthy people around us. not inclined to see uncleanliness in our homes, cities, or country. No one wishes for illness or the loss of a loved one; or to be considered inferior, or judged. we reject pollution, bad roads, traffic jams, war, and so on.

Nowadays, there are many things we wish to exchange as well. For example, people are rapidly changing their spouses, switching jobs, cities, societies, countries, names, religions has become very common.

These are all the significant considerations I've had so far. Now, let's delve into the micro-level of life. On a day-to-day or moment-to-moment basis, from morning to night, we act as if we are on a shopping trip. "I want to work out for one hour a day", "I want to arrive on time for the meeting", "I need to complete this target today", "I want to eat healthy food today", "or perhaps indulge in ice cream today". "I should aim for 9 hours of sleep". "I do not want to face my boss in a bad mood today." Sometimes, we feel confused. Should I study now or spend time with friends? It's too hot today, it's too cold today, and I do not want rain today since I have a birthday party in the open garden.

Additionally, shopping can be spiritual, as I seek peace and happiness. I want to recreate the experience I had on the retreat. I always strive to live in the present, and I want to discover who I am. I want to be a pure soul. I want to go on a higher conscious level after death This is shopping while embodying the identity of a spiritual seeker.

Experiencing a headache after reading all this? This is not a fictional life but our reality. The "money" we use for this shopping on Earth is "Information." Our minds can create a shopping list of desires and aversion based solely on the information we have gathered through our senses. Until we hear about a travel destination, we will never develop the desire to visit it. Until you encounter the term "enlightenment," you never wanted it. Thus, our shopping list is formed from the limited information our senses can perceive, and this information functions like money that generates a shopping list. We will never think of eating a fruit or dressing like the locals in Vietnam, for instance, until we visit Vietnam and experience it ourselves or receive that information from elsewhere. Therefore, we do not have room for magic. Magic signifies experiencing something without prior knowledge. Only then does the mind become surprised and enter an AWE state/mesmerized. We feel that if we live without a shopping list all the time, destiny has very little to offer, but in reality, it exceeds our expectations. If we stop perceiving this Earth as a shopping market, it does not imply that things will not come, be removed, or exchanged. Instead, you are at ease without a choice, and only the shopper dies, shopping continues as life goes on.

CHAPTER TWENTY ONE

HAPPINESS & GRACE OF TRUTH

I am real happiness. Then how can I show myself (i.e., happiness)? I am always here without cause, effect, action, reaction, situation or events.

I cannot create this ever-flowing undemanding happiness. But I can definitely obstruct it by the blocks of desires. The desires of what should happen when should happen? what is right and what is wrong, what is worthy and unworthy? These desires seem to create illusionary sorrow which is blocking happiness. for example, I create a desire that unless I get something I will not be happy. This something creates the illusion of sorrow that seems to block the ever-present happiness. Nature of this happiness is relaxation which is comparable to the calm trees in the forest. Its fragrance is peace having the depth of ocean ground. And its dress is awareness where every thought becomes naked and has no place to stand. This happiness is neither increasing not decreasing by adding or removing anything to it. It is just as it is. Can't be measured by any measurement unit. Its source is coming from the ever powerful "Nothing". This is not the negative nothing which mind imagines to be useless. But in fact, this nothing is the only source of everything happening in the sensory world.

Running for happiness is the first step to become unhappy. How can you achieve something which you already are?

My true confession is that; "I cannot explain this happiness neither can I express it in any form, I just know I am that".

 I can't be happy or unhappy because I am happiness originally.

Thank you for the grace to make me meet myself. I cannot possess this happiness but just be it.

Grace of Truth

Have you realized that sometimes you are chasing after something which seems very important to you but for some reason all your effort to get that thing goes in vain? And after a while you lose interest in chasing that very thing and forget about it completely. Suddenly one day you get that thing out of nowhere but at this time you have lost interest and happiness in getting it and have got a neutral perspective towards that thing. You will also realize that you cannot clearly define how you got that thing as you got it without any efforts or desire.

When you do not have a formula to get something in life and you are not working towards getting that something and still that thing happens to you, it is called as Grace. You must have listened to a quote "Grace is the only way!". This is true when the human being understands that his efforts are not bringing things in his life but rather something that he cannot answer is running his or her life blissfully, then he or she says it is all Grace. The things that are beyond logic, efforts and formula or a defined path to achieve it is called Grace. The moment I realize each and every happening in life is unplanned and is happening miraculously, my doer-ship wanes thinner and thinner and Grace free flows without any obstacle.

Maturity has occurred when you understand even challenges are grace as they arrive to show how foolishly you are planning life as life is running without your planning with full of love, peace and prosperity that one cannot even imagine.

Grace of love for Truth in true sense: - The logic behind

why some individuals are 16 years old but have deepest love for Truth and maturity to handle i.e., Sant Dnyaneshwar, Ramana Maharshi, Adi Shankaracharya because these souls are looking for Truth from thousands of years and marinated enough in seekers identity to the extent even to drop that identity. Whereas you see individuals, who do not have any inclination to Truth even if they turn 70 years of age. This is because these souls are in fact new souls and yet to complete their outer journey of desires to have and not to have. So do not compare with anyone; let every soul have its own path. Grace is same on all. Just trust your own path. Just don't stop saying thank you enough if by grace you have a single drop of inclination to know your true Self. Rarest grace is to be able to drop off the seeker's spiritual identity as well which seemed like a diamond dress you were wearing for thousands of years. Embrace the grace of "Nothing" which will drop off everything so that grace is only left!

<u>Thank you</u>

If there is any word left to describe life as it is; then that word is "Thank you!".

Thank you to the eyes for showing the grace, that is showered from the time these eye lids open in the morning to the time it closes at night.

The leaves of the plants glow in sunshine and tell good

morning every single day. The dew drops on the leaves, appear as tears of gratitude, thanking GOD for expressing through them.

The mechanism of breathing allows the same air which is present inside as well as outside the body to play the game of "hide and seek" with itself. Peace, love, abundance, gratitude, completeness, purity and satisfaction are the essence of 'every moment'.

Thank you for the 'oneness' that sparkles from the surrounding. People around me, plants, birds, animals and the non-living things; Everything has come up alive. They shine beyond there labels and just tell that I exist beyond any form.

Nothing is unique here but still every ordinary thing perceived as extra-ordinary, in itself.

Thank you for the magic unfolding moment by moment. Showing how life take care of life. The charioteer (Call him God, Self, Allah, Eshwar) of this life is unseen. As if This charioteer is riding the life on water.

Thank you for all the experiences taken through this body-mind and the ones that will never occur; However, the biggest thank you for this wisdom that there is no individual experiencer who is personally experiencing anything. All the experiences are created, experienced and destroyed by this charioteer itself and still it is untouched by any of them.

Thank you for the "Eureka moment!!" of the realization

that there is no "individual doer" who is running his/her
life rather life is taking care of life itself by the grace of
GOD. Touching the feet of this unknown that is driving
you into your own nature of limitless uncertainty.
Thank you for letting life know that life is happiness,
peace, freedom and meditation itself. Untouched by any
duality, without any strains or stars on its clothes.
Thank you for looking through this life "as it is". This
feels as if holy water splashed on eyes and removed the
dirt of millions of years. And so now the eyes are blank,
new and looking as the new born baby.
Thank you for the grace of wisdom that revealed,
 I am,
Dance & dancer but still nothing.
Paint & painter but still nothing.
Music & Musician but still nothing.
Creation & creator but still nothing.
First it felt like, dancer, painter, musician & creator are
illusion but now got to know dance, painting, music and
creation are also illusion. And left with only factual
experience of "Nothing", which cannot be created,
imagined, owned or destroyed.
Thank you for this "Nothing". This is the biggest gift of
life. This is the goal, meaning and life itself.
Thank you to the word "**thank you**" itself that gives the
opportunity to express this boundless gratitude to the
never-ending grace for which the tears of happiness

rolling down the eyes throughout this bodily life is not even a drop in ocean.